Beginners' Guide to Raspberry Pi

A Well-illustrated Guidebook to Learn about Raspberry Pi

Table of contents

Introduction

With the aim of enhancing the productivity of education, Eben Upton with his equals introduced an effective and low-cost device. This credit card-sized microcomputer inspired by the 1981 BBC Micro improved the programming skills as well as the enhancing better understanding of the computer hardware at pre-university level. The idea to develop this technological microcomputer arose after the by then Cambridge students realized that the pre-university students of the 1990's did not have the essential computer science and coding skills to gain much from this field of study. This was characterized by the rise of games and home PC that replaced the BBC Micros, Commodore 64 machines and Amigas among other programs.

To further the work by Eben Upton and colleagues, the Raspberry Pi Foundation charity. With their tireless efforts, the first-generation Raspberry Pi was released into the market in the year 2012 with the latest and third release (the Raspberry Pi 3.0) let into the market in February 2016. Ever since their 2012 when the device was introduced into the market, about eight million gadgets have been sold globally and hence making it a sure bet for its lovers. This has been boosted by the device's low cost and versatility. This was according to Pi Foundation reports.

Just like any computer, you can use the electronic to operate all the operation that any low-power computer has the ability to perform. This ranges from watching movies to playing games to writing documents among several other important and memorable tasks. This, however, is possible after you effectively assemble all the hardware. It is, therefore, important to have all the information on the various accessories as well as to assemble them for a memorable experience with your device. This helps the user to customize his or her device to hardware and software of his or her individual preference.

Preloaded with compilers and interpreters for different programming languages, this device is efficient for learning by the children and new users who have the interest in computing practices. To enhance the experience of the users, the Pi Foundation, just as indicated above, introduces new models with improved features in order to counter the limitations experienced in the preceding model.

It is also important to understand how to install the various operation systems such as the Linux effectively for a memorable application of this technological invention by the bright Cambridge students.

Just like the other single board computers (SBCs), the Raspberry Pi has the general-purpose input/output (GPIO) capabilities. This makes the device more preferable to both the laptops and desktop PCs that lacks the property.

As a shortcut to access all, the above tricks and operation steps, this book provides all the relevant information and therefore an effective starter kit for those who need to experience the gadget for the first time. The chapters of this book are clearly highlighted for easy understanding of its content and hence boosting the efforts towards making the world a global society through the enhancement of technology.

Always be on the frontline when it comes to technology. Rush to any nearby dealer, therefore, and acquire a computer at a cost-friendly price. This will allow you to enjoy the various computing programs that are important for the better understanding of the STEM subjects in the education system today (Science, Technology, Engineering, and Mathematics).

A photo of the Model A Raspberry Pi Board

CHAPTER ONE: Understanding the Raspberry Hardware

Just like any other PC, the Raspberry Pi comprises of features that define it. These include the following: CPU, GPIO pins, GPU, program memory, UART, power source connector, Xbee socket and Ethernet port. In addition to all these specifications, the device includes several other interfaces that allow for connection with external gadgets for a lively computer experience.

To begin enjoying the value of your money, the Raspberry Pi has all its features, including an Irvine-based Broadcom chip at the core of its board exposed. This allows the users to hook up his or her device to the external gadgets like the mouse, monitor, keyboard, and the internet among others for a complete computer experience.

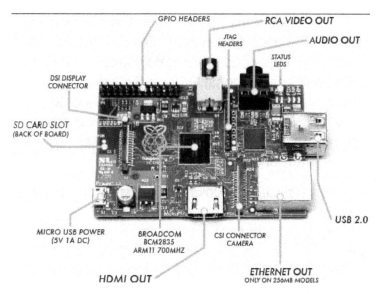

Hardware specification of the Raspberry Pi

To run its software, the device uses an inexpensive Secure Digital storage cards. The SD memory card as a mass storage to allow the Raspberry Pi to reboot just the same way the normal PCs boot up into their windows from their hard disks.

1. Memory

One of the reasons why Raspberry Pi is considered a low-power computer is its less memory capacity of between 256MB and 512MB. This is less compared to the PCs' RAM memories that are available in gigabytes. Because of this, the device is limited to low-powered programming operations. To boost the memory of the Raspberry Pi gadget, however; the default operating system recommends a minimum of 8GB SD card.

The SD card becomes useful to you the moment you load into it the operating system. Specific techniques to do this are explained in the next chapter of this updated and comprehensive book. To keep the software updated, it is a necessity for the user to update the SD card regularly. This ensures that your projects run smoothly. This updating process requires an active internet connection.

The computer will slow down once the SD card space becomes full. Checking the space available is, therefore, important to avoid this inconvenience when in the process of exploring the ever-advancing technology. In the process of freeing the space for a faster experience, the user will be forced to delete some of his or her content stored in the mass storage card.

Raspberry Pi New Out Of Box Software (NOOBS) microSD Card and SD Card Adapter — Debian Jessie

The recommended operating system for the Raspberry Pi is the Raspbian. With the SD card, however, the user is able to install different other operating systems such as the Pidora, RaspBMC, RISC OS, Arch Linux and OpenElec among others.

Because of the reality that not all the SD cards available in the market have the same failure rates, it is advisable for the Raspberry lovers to purchase the official SD cards from either Farnell or RS dealers.

2. The Graphics Processing Unit (GPU)

To enable the 3D experience, including the image calculation operation, the Raspberry Pi board includes a functional GPU. This allows for the effective display of the images on your monitor. To do this, the single-chip processor creates illumination effects (through mathematically intensive procedures) and hence transforming the objects whenever a 3D prospect is redrawn.

The CPU having been let off its primary role remain with free cycles that allow for it to perform other important functions that enhance the experience of the Raspberry owner.

In association with the CPU, however, the GPU accelerates the deep learning engineering and analytics applications. This is done when the GPU offloads some compute-intensive portions of the software applications off the CPU. As a result, the user's experience is enhanced.

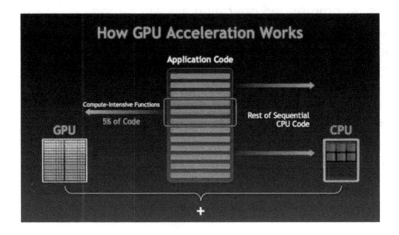

To boost its usefulness, the GPU includes a Broadcom video core IV as well as supports the OpenGL.

3. The ARM 11 Central Processing Unit (CPU)

This is considered the brain of the Raspberry Pi board. This feature, located at the System on the Chip, is responsible for facilitating the instruction by the computer via either mathematical or rather the logical operations.

As the GPU handles the operations for the graphic output, the CPU, on the other hand, handles all the other computing responsibilities including taking input, performing the calculation and producing output as a result.

Other than the memory, the CPU defines what a computer is. This two hardware are responsible for all the input, processing as well as the output operation in a computer.

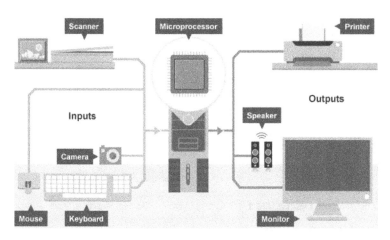

Labels in the figure: Scanner, Microprocessor, Printer, Outputs, Inputs, Speaker, Camera, Mouse, Keyboard, Monitor

Both the CPU and memory operate simultaneously to run computer programs through the fetch-decode-execute cycle.

To help the unit perform its functions effectively such as moving data from one memory location to the other, the CPU has three parts: Arithmetic logic unit (ALU), the control unit (CU) and the registers. Each of the parts has its individual functions. For example, the ALU works on the functions involving calculation while the control unit moves data via the processor when the register accommodates values for both the ALU and controller. The register is also important in changing values required to execute instructions.

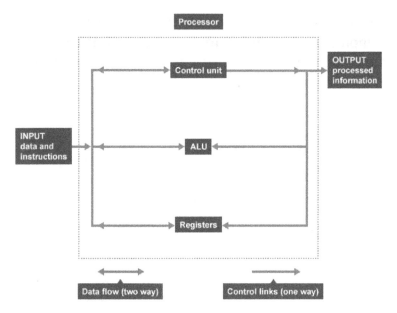

The main parts of the Central Processing Unit (CPU).

The ARM11 processor used by the Raspberry Pi ranks as much as the Samsung Galaxy devices and hence making the cheap computer a valuable purchase.

4. The GPIO Pins

To enable the credit-sized device to associate effectively with the other electronic boards such as the monitor for a smooth input and output commands, both the input and output pins are the essential component of the Raspberry Pi hardware. Because of this, the pins are considered the physical interface between the Raspberry Pi and the external world.

These pins are located along the edge of the board and next to the video out socket (yellow in color).

The GPIO pins are located along the edge of the board and next to the yellow video out socket.

However, out of the 26 pins along the board edge, only 17 of them are GPIO. The remaining 9 are either the ground or power pins. It is, therefore, important to have the full understanding to distinguish between the pins to avoid inconveniences.

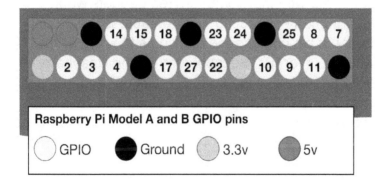

Identification of the 17 GPIO pins out of the 26 displayed.

By default, the GPIO pins go unused with no predefined function. With the desire of a system integrator to build a complete system, however, he or she requires the digital control line (the GPIO pins).

Connecting your Raspberry to the outside world using the GPIO pins has made it easy for the device holders to be able to control a number of activities at their own comfort. That is, with the Pi connected to an active internet connection, the user can control all the devices connected to the Raspberry from anywhere with the devices sending data back automatically.

When we utilize a GPIO stick as an output, each stick can turn on or off, or go HIGH or LOW in registering terms. At the point when the stick is HIGH it yields 3.3 volts (3v3); when the stick is LOW, it is off.

Unlike the GPIO output, input is somewhat trickier in light of the way that computerized gadgets work. Unconfirmed connecting a button across the ground and input pin confuse the device as to whether the switch is on or not. Because of this, the Raspberry Pi GPIO tutorials include both the "pull up" and the "pull down" phrases to help the user confirm in case of a received input.

5. The Ethernet Port

Although not featuring on the Raspberry Pi Zero because of the relatively space of the device compared to the other releases and cost, the Ethernet port is an important inclusion especially for those who desire to use their credit-card-sized electronic as a gaming darling. This port allows for communication with other devices by plugging your home router to an active internet connection.

For a faster internet connection, a direct Ethernet connection is preferred. This allows you to bypass your slow local network.

Raspberry Pi

Direct Ethernet Connection

For the holders of the Pi Zero device, it is possible to add an external Ethernet port the help of the SPI pins on your board. This involves careful wiring, Pi booting, tweaking of a config.txt line, enabling of the SPI and then rebooting of the device. Using the same SPI enables the user to get additional Ethernet ports in their desire to create either a home server or router from a Raspberry Pi without the need to using the local network like the Wi-Fi.

6. The Power Source Connector

To enjoy the experience by your valuable electronic board, an external power source is mandatory. For the earlier Pi models, a power supply of as low as 1.2A is advisable. This is unlike the latest Raspberry Pi 3 that requires about 5V, 2.5A power supply.

To power the device, therefore, the many mobile chargers (5V micro USB charger) can be used to power the Raspberry Pi under close monitoring to ensure they provide sufficient voltage as well as the current of up to 5V/1.2-1.25A in the case of the Pi 3 model. Many other devices such as the wall sockets with USB ports remain useful power source using the micro USB cables. Other than the wall sockets, the USB hubs, battery packs, and computers are alternative power sources.

However, to relieve yourself of the pressure the official Raspberry Pi power supply is recommended to provide the ample energy for your device.

An official Raspberry Pi power supply.

The Raspberry Pi device has a small switch on the side of the shield to allow for the connection of the external power source.

7. UART (Universal Asynchronous Receiver/ Transmitter)

This is a serial input and output port that is helpful in case of the need to transfer the serial information as a text. This is also useful in the conversation of the debugging code.

8. The XBee Socket

To allow your Raspberry Pi to communicate wirelessly with the help of the Zigbee (XBee). Setting up this hardware involves a simple plugging of the XBee module into your device through the XBee socket.

Plugged XBee module through the socket.

9. The HDMI connector

To connect your Raspberry Pi to your living room TV for a memorable experience, the HDMI connector provides a digital audio/video output. This is only possible with the help of the HDMI cable that connects your Pi to the HDMI-compatible television.

This port also allows for effective configuring of your Raspberry after booting it for a faster experience.

The HDMI cable

Of the 1.3 and 1.4 HDMI versions supported by the compatible external devices, the 1.4 version cable is preferred to the other for its reliability. This also allows you to enjoy your experience on a bigger screen.

For a computer experience, several other equipment such as a mouse (either wired or unwired) and a monitor accompanied with the correct adapter and cable. The Wi-Fi antennae port is also included to allow for connectivity to an active internet connection.

CHAPTER TWO: Getting started with the Raspberry Pi

With the knowledge about the specific components helpful for the computer-based endeavors, it is now time to set up your Raspberry Pi for the memorable experience that led to the invention of this technological device. This set up procedure is mandatory since the device does not come with peripherals such as the mouse, monitor or cables. To make this easier for the new users of this gadget, NOOBS allows setting up of the device in the absence of a reliable network access and without the need to download any special software.

1. Reformatting the microSD card

With all the items within your reach, the first step involved is reformatting the microSD card that provides the platform for the downloading of the operating system. Reformatting is mandatory since most of the SD cards bought contain extraneous files in them that need to be removed from the storage capacity.

To do this, insert first your microSD card into the USB card reader or adapter before connecting it to your computer.

The next step involves downloading the SD Formatter 4.0. Before formatting the card, confirm first that the memory card is compatible with your device. To do this, **double-click upon the SDFormatter_4.00B.pkg** located in the **Downloads folder** in your **Dock** for the installation of this feature.

Follow, therefore, the popping instruction in the installation window to see the process to the end.

From the **Dock**, tap on the **Launchpad** icon that resembles a silver rocket ship before finding the SD Formatter 4.0 app that had been downloaded earlier. To move between the Launchpad windows, however, tap on the **Next Page** options located on the lower part of the screen. Alternatively, this can be done by swiping either to the right or left using your Magic Mouse or the trackpad.

From here, touch the **SD Formatter 4.0** app to open a formatting window on your desktop

Locate the **Select Card** and tap on your microSD card from the drop-down menu. From the bottom right corner, tap **Format**. Upon the completion of the reformatting, a notification window appears. Click **OK** to close the window.

2. Downloading the NOOBS to the microSD

This is the next step for the beginners immediately after reformatting your SD card. To perform this, the card must be connected to the computer.

Download the ZIP file of the NOOBS Version 2.3. This easy operating system contains Raspbian and provides an alternative operating system. Avoid, however, the NOOBS Lite since it does not include the pre-loaded Raspbian.

From the **Downloads folder** in your **Dock**, click on the **NOOBS file**. After opening this NOOBS folder, tap the **first file** located inside it.

Navigate down and then **Shift + left - click** on the **last file** in the NOOBS folder.

Onto your desktop, drag and drop all selected NOOBS files into the SD card icon without having to open the SD card drive.

Once this is done, right-click on the **SD card icon** and then tap on the **Eject [SD Card Name]** to remove the card from either the card reader or the card adapter from the computer.

Complete the process by removing the microSD card from the reader.

3. Setting up your Raspberry Pi

With all the peripherals available, it is required that you plug in your Raspberry Pi to begin enjoying its features.

To begin with, insert your SD card into the card slot located on the underside of the Raspberry Pi.

Card slot on the underside of the board.

Once this is done, plug both the USB keyboards and the USB mouse into the two adjacent USB ports located on the Raspberry Pi.

Both the USB mouse and the USB keyboard are connected to the USB ports.

Alternatively, the user can opt to connect a Bluetooth adapter into one of the USB ports.

Once this is done, toggle on your HDMI-compatible TV or a monitor. Ensure it is set to the proper input (HDMI 1 or Component). With one end of the cable plugged into the Pi, plug into the monitor the HDMI or video component cable.

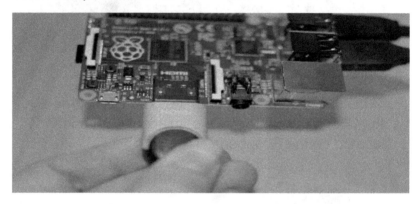

One end of the cable is plugged into the HDMI port on the Raspberry Pi board.

With the desire to connect to the internet, use an Ethernet cable to your router with the other end of the cable plugged into the Pi. Alternatively, the user can opt to connect the Wi-Fi adapter to the Raspberry Pi.

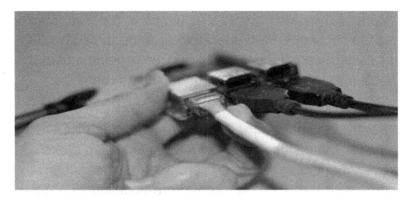

One end of the HDMI cable is plugged into the Ethernet port next to the two USB ports.

The next step involves connecting your Raspberry Pi to a reliable power supply. To do this, plug the power supply into via the power outlet to automatically toggle on and boot up the Pi.

Power indicator light confirms that the connection is complete.

4. **Downloading and installation of the operating system**

With all the hardware now assembled, the Raspbian is the recommended operating system, to begin with. This is because it is easy to use and contains useful software that helps in the conduction of many computer projects.

For the beginners, the earlier creation of the NOOBS makes the installation even much easier. To make it even more convenient to them, the new users can purchase the SD card with the pre-installed NOOBS.

After a successful connection of your computer system, a start screen displays on your monitor to begin the installation process.

The first step involves selecting the **Raspbian**. Once this is selected, tap **Install**.

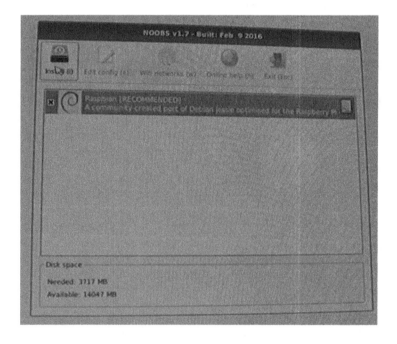

Select the recommended Raspbian operating system

Immediately after clicking the Install option, a warning window displays to inform you that with the help of an uncompressed version of the Raspbian operating system your microSD card will be overwritten. Tap **Yes** to allow the installation process to complete, and the Raspbian automatically boot.

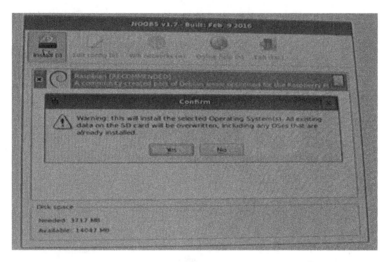

A warning window appears on the screen

5. Configuring your Raspberry Pi

Once booting of the Raspbian is complete, the Rasbian Home screen displays on the monitor's screen. This alerts you on the need to configure your Raspberry Pi system in order to add your personal information such as the date, location and time.

To perform this operation, the first step involves clicking the **Menu** located on the top left corner of the display.

Menu on the top left corner of the display

From the options that displays, navigate the drop-down menu and then click the **Preferences**.

Select the Preference option in the dropdown.

Under the Preference, click on the **Raspberry Pi Configuration** option

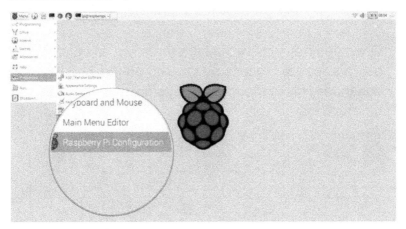

Display of the Raspberry Pi Configuration

Upon tapping on the **Raspberry Pi Configuration** option, a configuration window displays. Select the **Localisation** tab.

From the three options that appear, click on the **Set Locale** in order to set your location, **Set timezone** to set your local time and the **Set Keyboard** to set your keyboard language.

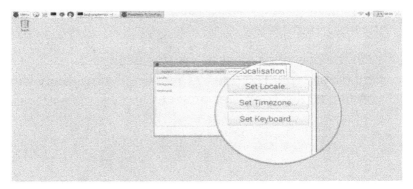

Options displayed upon clicking on the Localisation tab.

Once you have clicked all the three options displayed, begin a reboot process by tapping on the **Yes** icon to continue. This is the final step involved in the setting up process.

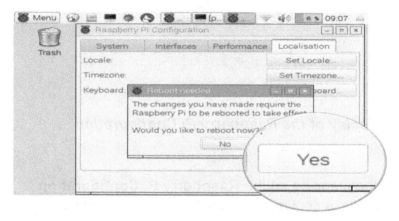

Click Yes to begin rebooting your Raspberry Pi.

The above procedure involved in the installation of the operating system is for the newbies. Most of the long-term users write the image of the Operating system to their SD card.

With the operating system now installed and configured, your Raspberry Pi device is now ready to conduct all the computer-project.

CHAPTER THREE: The Best of Raspberry Pi Projects

The prime purpose of the invention of Raspberry Pi was to help in the easier understanding of the computer hardware at pre-university level. Once it was introduced into the market, enterprising hobbyists discovered that the device could be handy in several other functions as well.

Because of this discovery, the Raspberry Pi has remained to be a valuable piece of tech that has ever been introduced into the market. The introduction of new models by the dealers is aimed at enhancing the value of this palm-fitting computer.

Regardless of whether you are a beginner or a tech veteran, this device is fantastic when it comes to fulfilling some of your computer-based projects. The prime purpose of this chapter, therefore, is to explain some of the important projects that the technologists have found the device useful. Ever since the introduction of the Raspberry Pi into the market in the year 2012, the device has been put to work on several projects ranging from practical to eccentric.

A. Networking your printers with the Raspberry Pi

Because of the importance of the printers in an office, most of the small offices are fitted with good non-network printers. This is because of the extra cost required for the acquisition of the more effective networked printing machines.

With regard to this, however, technicians have discovered a more pocket-convenient way of enjoying your hand-made networked printers within your personal offices. This project using the Raspberry Pi allows the office owner to upgrade their old printer into a "smart" printer.

Setting up this project is not a walk in the park since it requires software skills. This should not deny you sleep. To effectively see this project to completion, your printer has to be supported by a piece of software known as the Common Unix Printing System (CUPS). To confirm whether this software supported by your printing machine, visit the CUPS website and clear your doubts.

To kick-start, this project, one require the Raspberry Pi, Ethernet cord, a USB Printer and a micro SD card. The USB Keyboard, USB mouse, and the Raspberry Pi case are other optional items that can be made available. This procedure entails setting up of both the CUPS as well as the SAMBA.

For those who are not sure of the procedure to follow in facilitating this project, consult those experienced in conducting the endeavor.

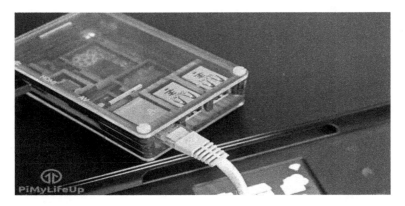

Functioning Raspberry Pi for a networked printer

B. Creation of a wireless extender using a Raspberry Pi

With your Raspberry Pi, the USB Wi-Fi dongle and a microSD card, it is possible to set up a wireless connection for convenient browsing all day long.

Turning your Raspberry Pi into a Wi-Fi Access Point has a number of benefits such as the creation of a free Access Point, creation of a Raspberry Pi Wi-Fi Hotspot, an extension of the existing Wi-Fi network and enhancing a closed Wi-Fi monitoring unit.

A created wireless extender using a Raspberry Pi.

C. Creation of a disposable GIF camera

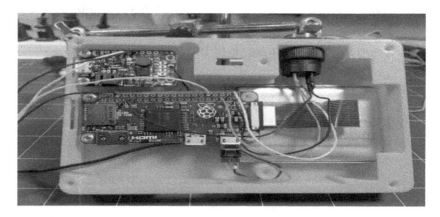

A Pix-E disposable camera by Nick Brewer

With the changing tradition, most of the people prefer watching the animated gifts to the videos. Because of this, Nick Brewer opted to create a camera that was helpful in the creation of the animated gifts.

To enable this, a combination of software ranging from GraphicsMagick, PiCamera, and the GifCam proved to turn into a valuable machine for taking such animations for sharing with friends. The camera has a 3D-printed enclosure that only becomes valuable when additional hardware like a pack of battery, an illuminated push button, and an Adafruit Powerboost 500 charge controller are other important equipment for the success of this project.

The Pi's SD card is accessible without having to disassemble the camera. In case the battery power reduces, charging is through the USB port.

To achieve this, soldering, engineering, and breadboarding skills are required to meet this success in this project.

D. Setting up of a Media Centre for your TV using a Raspberry Pi

Through the HDMI ports found in the Raspberry Pi, it is possible for the user to set up the device to be his or her home media center. Plug one end of the HDMI cable into the HDMI port with the other end connected to the TV set. This allows the user to be able to access all the media, without having to fork out for the Apple television.To make the project easier, specific operating systems such as the RasPlex and the Raspbmc are built to access the remote media from other locations. This will only be possible when you are connected to an active internet connection such as the Wi-Fi controlled through remote apps on the user's smartphone.

A Raspberry Pi-customized Media Centre for your TV

E. Building a download hub using your Raspberry Pi

To avoid spending a frustrating amount of our time downloading content from the internet because of poor internet signals, it is advisable for the users to route their downloads through a Raspberry Pi to the external storage device.

Using the Raspberry Pi as a dedicated hub for all streams, torrents among other downloads help in freeing the computer memory improving the processor speed.

Using the Raspberry Pi allows all the downloading processes to complete

Among the other projects that can be made possible with the help of the Raspberry Pi includes the following:

- ➤ Creation of a dedicated Minecraft machine
- ➤ Building of a camera trap
- ➤ Making of solar smart meter
- ➤ Building a lamp that changes color basing on the weather forecast
- ➤ Setting up of a home surveillance system for security reasons

Acquire the cheap and reliable Raspberry Pi to enjoy all the projects that are made possible with this excellent device.

CHAPTER FOUR: Differences between the Raspberry Pi Models

Ever since the introduction of the Raspberry Pi in the year 2012, different manufacturers have revolutionized around the globe. By November 2016, there were up to seven different versions of the device crowding the market. Though this was advantageous to win the market world, it has proved to be a headache for the new users of the device in selecting the best model that will satisfy their individual desires. This confusion arises since some of the Pi boards are almost identical to select at a glance.

Pictured from left to right: Raspberry Pi 1, 2 and 3.

This chapter, therefore, aims at familiarizing the lovers of this palm-size computer with the various available models to make it easy for them to select for any project they might desire to carry out. This ranges from the physical variations, the performance rate, the specs variations and the operating systems working on the different Raspberry Pi models. A new model introduced into the market comes with additional features that make the utilization by the owner memorable.

Despite the variations in the features defining the different Raspberry Pi models, the following functions are similar across all the versions:

- ❖ They can work with the Raspbian RaspBMC, Arch Linux, OpenELEC Pidora operating systems.
- ❖ All the features have the HDMI Composite RCA.
- ❖ They all utilize the Micro USB as the main power source.
- ❖ They have a supported resolution of between 640x350 and 1920x1200, including THE 1080p, PAL as well as the NTSC standards.

1) Defining features of the Raspberry Pi Zero

The Raspberry Pi Zero model is almost half the size of the Model A+, but with twice the utility. For easy identification of this small and affordable version of the Pi for your projects, the following are features that define this useful board:

- ✓ It comes with a 1Ghz, single-core CPU
- ✓ The board comes with a memory of 512MB RAM.
- ✓ Comes with both the mini HDMI and USB On-The-Go ports

- ✓ A CSI camera connector, with v1.2 only.
- ✓ Includes both the video and the reset headers.
- ✓ Comes with a micro USB power port.
- ✓ A 40-pin header that is HAT-compatible.

The above are the basic features that can be used to identify this model of the Pi board.

2) The defining features of the Raspberry Pi Model A+

This model replaced the original Model A in the year 2014. The version is the low-cost variant of the Raspberry Pi and compares from the Model A considering the following features:

- This version comes with more GPIO pins. In addition to the 26 pins in the Model A and B, the GPIO header has grown to about 40 pins.
- Comes with switched regulators unlike the previous linear regulators on the Model A. this enables it to save much energy by consuming power ranging from 0.5W to 1W.
- Unlike the initial SD socket, this version comes with a micro SD version that is easy to insert into the board.
- The incorporation of a dedicated low-noise power supply enhances the audio quality of this Pi model.
- Alignment of the USB connector with the edge of the board, additional four squarely-placed mounting ports as well as the moved composite video onto the 3.5mm jack enhances its aesthetic value.

This small (about 2cm shorter than the Model A) is appropriate for embedded projects that require lesser power as well as the Ethernet or rather the USB ports.

3) Defining features of the Raspberry Pi 1 Model B+

This Raspberry Pi model is the final revision of the original Pi. This replacement of the Model B has features similar to the Raspberry Pi 1 Model A+ except that has four USB 2.0 ports. This is different from the two found on the Model B.

4) The Raspberry Pi 2 Model B

This model is the second generation Raspberry Pi that came after the Raspberry Pi Model B+. To show how different it is from the previous Raspberry Pi 1, this device features the following properties:

- This board comes with a 900MHz quad-core ARM Cortex-A7 CPU.
- It has a 1GB RAM unlike the 512MB RAM of the Raspberry Pi 1.

Despite the slight differences, the device includes the following additional features that are as well found in the Raspberry Pi 1 Model B+:

✓ Includes an HDMI port
✓ Four USB ports
✓ Comes with up to 40 GPIO pins.

- ✓ A VideoCore IV 3D graphics core
- ✓ A micro SD card slot
- ✓ Includes both the camera interface (CSI) and the display interface (DSI).
- ✓ A combined 3.5mm audio jack as well as the composite video.
- ✓ An Ethernet port.

Because of the device's ARMv7 processor, the device has the ability to run a variety of operating systems like the Snappy Ubuntu Core, Linux distributions as well as the Microsoft Windows 10.

The Raspberry Pi 2 is believed to be compatible with the Raspberry Pi 1 because of its close identity with the Pi 1 Model B+.

5) Unique features of the Raspberry Pi 3 Model B

This is the third generation Raspberry Pi model. This 2016 release has the following features that define it:

- ➢ It introduces an 802.1n Wireless LAN.
- ➢ Comes with a 1.2GHz bit quad-core ARMv8 CPU.
- ➢ A Bluetooth 4.1 as well as a Bluetooth Low Energy (BLE).
- ➢ It comes with a 1GB RAM.
- ➢ 40 GPIO pins.
- ➢ The port includes about four USB ports.
- ➢ A micro SD card slot.
- ➢ Both the camera interface (CS) and the display interface (DSI).

- ➢ A full HDMI port.
- ➢ Introduces a combined 3.5 mm audio and the composite video.
- ➢ An Ethernet port.

This model is compatible with both the Raspberry Pi 1 and 2 because of its identical forms to the previous PI 1 model B+ and the Pi 2.

Regardless of the similarities with the previous Pi 1 and Pi 2, the Raspberry Pi 3 is 65% faster than the Pi 2.

When idle, the power of the Pi 3 drops from 900MHz to 600MHz. This means that it consumes less power compared to the previous releases.

6) The latest Raspberry Pi 4

According to the Raspberry Pi Foundation, this upgrade of the Model B is the last release until 2019 with the aim of boosting its workability. For example, this 2017 model come with an upgraded 64-bit processor.

To make it even more reliable and in touch with the current technology, Google Company partner with the Foundation to bring the artificial intelligence (AI) and the machine learning tools into this outstanding microcomputer.

This Pi release shares some common features as the preceding models. However, the following features make it unique as well as more reliable compared to the earlier releases:

- An upgraded BCM4908 processor that boosts the processing power from 1.2GHz to 1.8GHz.
- Comes with USB 3 ports aimed at enhancing quality power management as well as boosted transfer speeds.
- The Raspberry Pi has a 2GB RAM.

It is, therefore, important to consider having the knowledge of all these Pi versions before selecting the best one for your project.

A picture of the Raspberry Pi 4's special features

CHAPTER FIVE: Getting More Out Of the Raspberry Pi

With the various models of the Raspberry Pi, the user can see to completion his or her personal projects. To enhance this productivity. However, initial setting up the process of the Pi is mandatory, including the writing programs, and operating systems among other useful procedures to ensure your device works perfectly.

For the benefits of new users, this chapter includes information about the Linux operating system, the Python program, and the Exodus Kodi add-ons that are aimed at boosting the functions of this excellent product of the Raspberry Pi Foundation. For example, the Exodus add-on allows the user to watch a selection of live channels with the Python program help in the automation of tasks such as the movement of bulk files among others to make the Pi valuable.

For this reason, it is essential for both the newbies and the long-term lovers of this microcomputer to take time and go through the information hereinbefore opting to run the programs, operating systems or even the add-ons on their Pi purchases.

A. Raspberry Pi and the Python program

One of the reasons why Eben Upton decide to invent this microcomputer was to enhance programming lessons among the pre-university students. The programming aspect of this great discovery is helpful for most of the new Raspberry Pi users for effective understanding of the specific language of the system.

Putting much attention on the new users of the Raspberry Pi and the involved programs, the Python is highly recommended as a language easily understandable. Because of this, the latest Raspbian operating system comes preloaded with the Python (the official programming language of both the IDLE 3 and Raspberry Pi.

The programs are similar to the shell scripts (files contain a series of commands executed by the computer from top to bottom).

This program is text-based meaning that you can apply any text editor with the aim of creating a program.

It is, therefore, important for the user to have the special information for the effective writing of this easy to understand Python program. For example, it is required that you install the Python interpreter on your PC to run the program since it does not require compiling.

a) Procedures for writing and running a program in Python

The Raspbian operating system comes pre-installed with both the Python 2.x and the Python 3.3. The Python 3.x being the latest version of the Python language, it is required that the user updates the program before running the program on the Raspberry Pi.

The first step involves opening the IDLE 3 application. This involves double-clicking the **IDLE 3** icon on the LXDE desktop. Alternatively, the user can tap the **desktop menu** located on the lower left side of the screen then choose the **Programming→IDLE 3**. This set up takes several seconds for a window with interactive triple chevron (>>>) displayed on the left side of the screen. This is an indication that the interpreter is waiting for your commands. To start a new Python program, therefore, choose the **File→New Window**. This selecting of the File→New Window follows a script-editing window on the right.

From the displayed script-editing window, key in the below text in the new window:

```
#my first Python program
username = input("Hello, I'm Raspberry Pi! What is your name? ")
print ('Nice to meet you, ' + username + ' have a nice day!')
```

From this point, click the **File** followed by **Save As**. In the new dialogue window that pops up, rename your file "hello" and the tap **"Save."**

To run the written Python program, click **Run** followed by **Run Module**. Alternatively, you can simply press **F5**. This prompts the "Hello, I'm Raspberry Pi! What is your name?" in the IDLE 3 window. From here, type your name before pressing **Enter** and wait for the Raspberry Pi to respond.

Using the Python programming language, many applications that are more powerful can be written into the Raspberry Pi.

With the Python program in your Raspberry Pi, you can conduct the various projects toward enhancing your computing experience.

B. Raspberry Pi and LINUX

For a computer to run effectively, an operating system has to manage the communication between both the hardware and the software. The Windows XP, Windows 7, Mac OS X, Windows 8 and Linux are some examples of the software that enhances the association between the sets of features in a PC.

Linux is the best of all considering its reliability as well as the zero cost of entry. This means that you can install this software on as many PCs as possible without paying a cent. This OS comes with a variety of versions (distribution) to fit the different users' preferences: Linux Mint, Ubuntu Linux, Arch Linux, Debian Linux (Raspbian) and the Feroda among several other software. Nearly all these distributions can be downloaded without having to pay for them.

For the Raspberry Pi, Raspbian is the recommended operating system for the newbies because it comes pre-installed with a variety of software helpful in programming, education among other useful computer operations. Such software includes the Python, Scratch, Mathematica, and Sonic Pi among others.

a. Linux Installation

The easy installation procedure is one of the reasons why this Linux is the recommended operating system for the new users. Because of the live distribution offer by most Linux versions, the software can be run from either a USB flash drive or a CD/DVD without having to make changes to the hard drive. Once you have transferred the software to the hard drive, you do not have to perform the installation.

Being the official operating systems by the Raspberry Pi Foundation, all the Pis support the Raspbian OS. The following are, therefore, the steps for the installation of the Raspberry Pi operating system image of the SD card of your Pi gadgets:

The first step involved in this procedure it to download the OS image. These images are available on the Raspberry Pi website Download page. This will be possible in the presence of an active internet connection.

After the download is complete, it is now time to write the image to the SD card. To do this, an image-writing tool has to be available to allow you install the images on your SD card. Etcher is an example of such writing tool that is known to work on the OS such as the Linux and the Windows. This writing tool allows writing of the images directly on the SD card without having to unzip them. To write the images using this tool, therefore, follow the steps below:

❖ First, download and install the Etcher on your computer.

- ❖ With the SD card connected with the SD card reader, open the Etcher then choose from your hard drive the Raspberry Pi *.img* or *.zip* file you wish to write on your SD card.
- ❖ Choose the SD card that you wish to write the selected image.
- ❖ Take your time to confirm your selection before tapping Flash to begin writing the data to the SD card of your choice.

N/B: For those who do not wish to use the Etcher, unzip the downloaded images to get the image file before writing it to your SD card.

Once this writing process is complete, boot your Pi device to turn it into the Raspbian operating system.

Alternatively, users can purchase the SD cards that are pre-installed with the official and latest Raspbian image.

C. Raspberry Pi and Exodus

Among the many advantages enjoyed by the Pi owners are the ability to stream and live channels and videos from the internet. This is enabled in case the Kodi app is installed on the computer. To facilitate this advantage, Lambda developed the Genesis add-on to facilitate your convenience when watching the TV shows, live channels or even movies by simply clicking a button.

Due to poor maintenance of the software, users began raising problems with their app. This called for the introduction of the Exodus add-on that is more convenient and with similar capabilities as the previous Genesis. With all this historical knowledge, it is important to install this add-on on your device's Kodi for a comfortable experience.

To install this software on your microcomputer, it is advisable to consider the direct install method:

> First, download the Exodus file directly on the Kodi. This is followed by launching the Kodi then tap on the **System** > **Add-ons** > **Install from zip file**.
> Upon clicking the **Install from zip file** option, locate your downloaded Exodus repository zip file then tap on it to install.
> From this point, go back to the Add-ons screen display and choose the **Install from repository** followed by **Exodus repository** > **Video Add-ons** and then finally choose **Exodus** to install it. Upon tapping the **Exodus** option, small message displays. Wait for the countdown to reach zero for the installation to be complete.

To confirm your installation, visit the **VIDEOS** folder then navigate to the **Video Add-ons** to locate Exodus among other add-ons.

Allow your Exodus add-on to play a video stream automatically based on the priority level defined in the HD/SD Host tabs. To customize this, click on the **VIDEOS** folder then navigate to **Video Add-ons** before right clicking the add-on to display options from which you should select **Add-on settings** then finally the **Playback** tab to enable all the settings that include the **Auto-play** inside them.

Enabling the subtitle support is also essential for the streaming experience. To do this, navigate to the rightmost tab and the tap Enable subtitles. From this stage, the user is advised to select the language of his or her choice.

CHAPTER SIX: Distinguishing the Raspberry Pi from the Arduino

Both the Arduino and the Raspberry Pi are the best single-board computers for your day-to-day projects. Selecting the best board for a specific project becomes difficult especially for the newbies. This includes the advantages that come with either board. It is for this reason that this chapter highlight exceptional comparisons between the two microcomputers.

 VS.

Visual comparison between the Arduino on the left and the Raspberry Pi on the left

Functional differences between the Arduino and the Raspberry Pi

Going by the functional definition between the two boards, an Arduino is defined as a microcontroller motherboard. This is because of its ability to run one program at a time. Raspberry Pi, on the other hand, is a general-purpose computer that makes use of the Linux operating system as well as its ability to run multiple programs.

Arduino, being a microcontroller, excels at controlling small machineries such as the motors, sensors, and lights. This makes it applicable in projects such as the building of a motion detector alarm and the likes.

Raspberry Pi, on the other hand, is more like a complete computer with its own operating system (only that it is slow in operations). With coding knowledge, therefore, the user is able to use it as a server to communicate with other PCs as well as serving as a Chromecast.

Selection of the effective board to use depends on what you desire the project to achieve. That is, for "lighter" projects you consider the Arduino while for the "bulky" one Raspberry Pi boards.

Hardware comparison between the Arduino and the Raspberry Pi

From just looking at the two boards, there are some slight differences noted. Let us see the differences basing on their power utilization, connectivity, I/O pins, USB and the storage.

1) Power

Because of the simple power requirement by the Arduino, a sudden power disconnection stops it automatically (no need to run a shutdown procedure).

The Raspberry, on the other hand, includes a full-featured computing system hence must be shut down just like any other computer. Power cuts can damage the microcomputer hence special care has to be taken.

Fortunately, both boards have very low power draw hence can be run for an extended period of the absence of electricity.

2) Connectivity

For internet connectivity, the Raspberry Pi includes a built-in Ethernet port. It is as well easy to locate a USB Wi-Fi dongle to award it a wireless connectivity. It is because of this reason that this board is preferred for starting of personal web servers, VPNs, and the printer servers.

Arduino, on the other hand, lacks the built-in connectivity capability. For an internet connection, therefore, an additional hardware that includes an Ethernet port is mandatory. This is the reason why this board, unlike the Pi, is meant for the hardware projects.

3) Input/Output Pins (I/O Pins)

For communication between your board and the things connected to it, the I/O Pins are helpful.

The difference comes considering the number of the pins on either board. The Raspberry Pi has about 17 pins while the Arduino includes up to 20 pins.

The temporal resolution to control the two boards differentiates them. Basing on CPU time, the Pi, for example, might have some difficulty in getting the timing down to a small fraction of a second because of complicated features. Arduino, on the other hand, has the ability to change the output as well as monitor the inputs on its pins down to a very limited time.

4) Storage

The Arduino includes up to 32 KB of onboard storage enough to store the code responsible for providing information for its running program. The Raspberry, on the other hand, lacks the onboard storage, but instead, it comes with a micro SD port to add as more storage capacity as you like.

5) USB

The Arduino does not come with standard USB ports for communication since it is not meant to communicate with other computers.

On the other hand, the Pi comes with four USB ports that can be used to connect it to either a router, an external hard drive, a printer or a variety of devices.

The software comparison between the Arduino and Raspberry Pi

The software differences depend on the functions of each board. Arduino, for example, does not come with any software because of its basic capabilities in interpreting the code that it receives while altering the hardware connected to it. The board lacks the operating system or any other form of interface other than the Arduino integrated development environment (IDE).

The Pi, on the other hand, includes a functional operating system known as Raspbian and a number of other useful apps to help in the completion of the project at hand.

With the information therein, it is vital to decide on the project you need to take part in before choosing on the board to acquire.

Conclusion

Following the need to improve both the coding and programming education among the pre-university students, Eben Upton invented Raspberry. This has ever since gained popularity among the global population with many of them using it to run some important and valuable computer projects.

Having the information about a product is one way of proving how valuable it is. For this reason, it is also important for the lovers of the Pi to understand all the defining features of the board to understand how handy it is. This includes the systematic procedure involved in setting it up for a memorable application. This will lead to knowledge in the various fields where this tech can be applicable to an enjoyable life.

This book includes all the vital information for effective utilization of the board. That is the specific features and the tricks required in order to get started with the microcomputer. In addition, this book includes a chapter that provides the differences between the Raspberry Pi and the Arduino boards that have been confusing to most of the new users. To make it even easy to grasp the content, this book includes some pictures to give the reader a better know-how about this important gadget.

For this reason, it is advisable for both the newbies and the long-term lovers of the Raspberry Pi to purchase this detailed copy in order to ensure they feel their value when it comes to conducting the many illustrated Pi projects.

Acquiring this book also provides the reader with some specific differentiating features between all the available versions of the Pi boards.

Do not be the one left behind regarding the coding and programming knowledge and the Pi in specific. Purchase this book and be up to date in the face of the whole world. This is a way of boosting the ever-advancing technology.

Finally, if you enjoyed this book, please take the time to share your thoughts and post a review on Amazon. It would be greatly appreciated! Thank you and good luck!